Experiencing
The Bible
Promises

How to Claim Your Rights
and Inheritance in Christ

2 Corinthians 1:20
"For all the promises of God in
him are yea, and in him Amen,
unto the glory of God by us."

Contents

CHAPTER ONE 7

Introduction 7

God Does Not Lie 8

A Big Lesson (Luke 1:1-80).......9

Promises, Grace and Faith.....12

A Promise is a Debt.................14

God's Promises are Reliable..16

God's Promises to You............17

CHAPTER TWO 21

The Promises We Can See 21

God is Merciful 23

Healing of the Body.................25

Divine Provisions.....................27

Divine Opportunities and
Financial Breakthrough..........29

Divine Protection and
Guidance 31

Summary.................................34

CHAPTER THREE 37

The Promises We Don't See................37

God's Spiritual Promises 40

Summary.................................66

CHAPTER FOUR......................................69

Why God Made Promises 69

CHAPTER FIVE..............................84

The Enemies of God's Promises 84

The Five Enemies of God's
Promises...................................86

Summary.......................................94

CHAPTER ONE

Introduction

Living in God's promises is one of the best places to be. Just like heaven, you enjoy the best that God has for you. People who make promises often are willing to fulfill them. When you receive a promise from someone, you do many things to get the attention of the other person. You wake up thinking of that promise. No day passes without a thought about it. You live every day to see that promise come to fulfilment.

Sometimes, you do some funny things to remind that person of the promise they made. You send morning, afternoon, or evening hello. You send cards on special days and do everything to get noticed and remembered. These well-intentioned actions may either annoy or impress the one who made a promise to you.

Humans may be offended when you remind them of the promises they made. They may even take back the promise due to your constant reminders. God doesn't do that. When God makes promises, He is always willing to fulfill them. A constant reminder impresses Him and moves Him to give you the things you need.

God Does Not Lie

When God makes a promise, it's His nature to fulfill it. God cannot lie and will not lie (Hebrews 6:18). As He was thousands of years ago, so He remains forever. People lie because of fear and weakness. They don't want to make other people angry. They feel they do not have what it takes to handle a bad situation. So they tell lies to escape punishment or to cover their inabilities or bad outcomes.

God does not fear anyone. He is the Most Powerful Person in the universe. Although He's a spirit, He can manifest in the flesh. God can do anything and can change unfavorable situations. That is why He does not lie. Lying is for those who have no power. God has unlimited power, so He says the truth at all times. Those who believe in the power of God to save and preserve life don't lie too.

A Big Lesson (Luke 1:1-80)

Zechariah and Elizabeth had no child and were already too old to have any. They continued serving God the best way they could despite their lingering and almost forgotten needs. One day, while in the temple of God, Angel Gabriel appeared to old Zechariah. "You are going to have a son named John," the excited angel announced.

The old man thought he heard wrongly. "What did you say? Did I hear you correctly? How could an old man and an old woman have a healthy child at this age?" Zechariah knew the promises of God. He also knew what God could do but he was thinking through his body and mind. He didn't focus on God's unfailing promises and His power to do all things.

"Dear Zechariah," Angel Gabriel patiently began, trying hard to hide his holy surprise at human unbelief. "This message doesn't come from me but from the Almighty and Eternal God, the Creator of heaven and earth. So your lack of faith isn't toward me but toward God. I thought that a man who knew so much about God and even taught other people would have a living faith. But I'm disappointed that your faith isn't up to one quarter of a mustard seed. Therefore, as soon as our discussion is over, you will lose your ability to speak until this promise comes to pass. If a teacher of God's word has no faith, he has no business telling others to have faith in God. So, God is taking away your ability to speak until you learn to practice what you preach."

And so Zechariah lost his speaking ability. He could only communicate through signs, symbols and writings. He could no longer say "I love you" to his wife, old Elizabeth. He couldn't say the traditional "good morning" to fellow priests, Levites and Israelites. His unbelief did him more harm than he had ever thought. Zechariah then realized that unbelief could keep someone in bondage without the person ever knowing it. He feared to imagine other areas he might have limited God and still couldn't discover them.

Promises, Grace and Faith
Romans 4:16
"Therefore it is of faith, that it might be by grace; to the end the promise might be sure to all the seed; not to that only which is of the law, but to that also which is of the faith of Abraham; who is the father of us all."

Grace is God's provision for you despite your sin, weakness and stubbornness. Faith is a strong belief in God and in what He can do. You need faith to open the door of God's grace. All of God's promises are stored in the grace rooms. If you don't have faith, you can't enjoy the fulfillment of God's promises. If you still doubt God's word, God cannot do anything good in your life. Faith is like a key. It is the key to God's promises. Everything we receive from God comes through grace. The benefits of grace are for people who believe. Grace and faith work together. The presence of one means the presence of the other. The absence of one is the absence of the other.

The riches of God's grace are His precious promises. You can access them through faith in God (Romans 3:24; Ephesians 2:8; Psalm 45:2). Some believers think that grace works on its own. They don't see the link between grace and faith. Grace brought down God's promises. Only a living faith in God can claim those promises

(Romans 5:2; 9:2; Galatians 3:14; Ephesians 3:12).

A Promise is a Debt

When God spoke to Abraham, He promised to bless him above everyone on earth. God made the same promise to Isaac and Jacob. When the Israelites grew in number, God still kept to His promise. He bound Himself with an irrevocable oath not to break His promises (Psalm 110:4). God has all the power to do the impossible, therefore He could do the impossible.

While Abraham lived, God fulfilled many promises. During the life of Isaac and Jacob, God continued to fulfill the promise He made to their father, Abraham. Abrahamic blessings were so full and rich that Abraham, Isaac and Jacob thought they had it all. But they merely tasted less than half of what God promised. No matter how long you live, you cannot exhaust the promises and blessings of God. That's why you must make efforts to enjoy as many promises as possible.

In Exodus, God raised Moses, Aaron and Miriam to lead all the Israelites out of Egypt. This was in fulfilment of the promise God had made to Abraham over four hundred years earlier. The Israelites themselves were waiting for the day when God would fulfil that particular promise. Although four hundred and thirty years went by, God didn't forget that promise. Even though Abraham who originally received the promises was dead, God didn't pretend He didn't make such a promise to his descendants.

Our God keeps to His promises. He doesn't make excuses of forgetfulness and fatigue. All He promised His people down through the ages, He fulfilled. He will fulfill everything He has promised you in Christ Jesus. God is no man's debtor. He never forgets His promises. Time and age do not affect His power or memory. He is ever fresh, ever active and ever faithful to His promises.

God's Promises are Reliable

Malachi 3:6

"For I am the Lord, I change not; therefore ye sons of Jacob are not consumed."

God does not change either in nature or power. He is reliable at all times, day and night. His promises have the same attributes. You can rest in God's promises. You can expect God to do as He promised. God is never too late in fulfilling His promises. Our impatience sometimes gets in our way and we think a promise is taking too long to manifest. We need to think the Bible way. Every promise has a specific time of manifestation and fulfilment.

When God promised Abraham and Sarah a son, He gave them a specific time. When He promised to give Abraham the land of Canaan, He told him it would be after his death. Abraham enjoyed his life so much that he felt like nothing could be more fulfilling than what he experienced. When the Israelites came into the Promised Land, they saw that the land indeed flowed with milk and honey. Abraham would have been humbled if he knew how Canaan looked like.

God's Promises to You

God's promises are for you and your loved ones (Acts2:39). God has promised to heal you, provide for your needs, save you from dangers and guide and protect you all through life. As He did it for Abraham, Isaac, Jacob and the Israelites, He will do it for you. There are thousands of promises in the Bible. You cannot exhaust them all but you can claim and enjoy as many as you can right now. Come to God in prayer and He will begin to open to you a new life of answered prayers and fulfillment of promises.

Psalm 2:8
"Ask of me, and I shall give thee the heathen for thine inheritance, and the uttermost parts of the earth for thy possession."

Ezekiel 36:36-38

"Then the heathen that are left round about you shall know that I the Lord build the ruined places, and plant that that was desolate: I the Lord have spoken it, and I will do it. Thus saith the Lord God; I will yet for this be enquired of by the house of Israel, to do it for them; I will increase them with men like a flock. As the holy flock, as the flock of Jerusalem in her solemn feasts; so shall the waste cities be filled with flocks of men: and they shall know that I am the Lord."

Matthew 7:11
"If ye then, being evil, know how to give good gifts unto your children, how much more shall your Father which is in heaven give good things to them that ask him?"

CHAPTER TWO

The Promises We Can See

Genesis 13:14-16
"And the Lord said unto Abram, after that Lot was separated from him, Lift up now thine eyes, and look from the place where thou art northward, and southward, and eastward, and westward: [15] For all the land which thou seest, to thee will I give it, and to thy seed for ever. [16] And I will make thy seed as the dust of the earth: so that if a man can number the dust of the earth, then shall thy seed also be numbered."

The promises of God covers the entire aspects of our lives: body, soul and spirit. Everything you need in life is found in God's promises. God made sure He caters for all our needs. If we need anything, we go to His word and take it. Some of these promises are for our physical lives (Exodus 15:26). God gave them to us because as our Creator, it is His duty to correct anything that goes wrong with our bodies.

In Genesis, the Bible revealed that God created man from the dust. God gave life to man by giving him the breath of life, and man came alive. While in the Garden of Eden, Adam and Eve had no physical defects. They were never sick or in pain. They had no headaches, heartaches or cramps in any part of their bodies.

God provided everything they needed for survival. There was surplus foods in the form of nourishing fruits. The weather was so nice that they needed no clothes. The man and the woman were naked and felt good about it. Their innocence was so pure that they had nothing to hide from God and each other.

Then came the devil, and tricked man to sin against God. When the man and the woman fell, they lost the physical blessings. God could no longer guarantee their health and wealth. Adam and Eve had to work hard to make ends meet. The period of free food and housing was over.

God is Merciful

The nature of God won't let Him to leave Adam and Eve in that condition. Even after disobeying Him, God still added a promise that one day someone born of the woman would crush the head of the enemy who brought sickness, suffering, pain and death to man's world.

To show that He cared, God's promises to heal and provide for our needs continued. God used prophets, kings and holy men and women to fulfill His promise to meet our physical needs. He was too merciful, gracious and compassionate to forget us (Isaiah 49:15; Psalm 137:5).

Throughout the Old Testament, God provided for and healed His people through Moses (Exodus 14:15-31; Exodus 16:13-23; Exodus 17:3-7; Numbers 11:30-32), Joshua (Joshua 3:7-17; Joshua 4:21-24; Joshua 6:20), and kings and prophets (1 Samuel 7:10-13; 17:45-51; 1 Kings 17:14-16; 18:41-45; 2 Kings 2:19-22; 5:1-19; 4:1-7)

God used Jesus Christ, His Son, to bring physical blessings to His people. Jesus, being God Himself, was so full of compassion that He healed everyone that came to Him. The blind, lame, deaf and dumb received their healings (Matthew 4:23; Mark 5:34; Luke 17:11-19; John 111-44). Even the hungry were fed by Jesus. God made sure that His promises remain reliable and true to His people (Matthew 8:17; 12:17-21).

Healing of the Body

"Who forgiveth all thine iniquities; who healeth all thy diseases," Psalm 103:3.

"He sent his word, and healed them, and delivered them from their destructions," Psalm 107:20.

"Who his own self bare our sins in his own body on the tree, that we, being dead to sins, should live unto righteousness: by whose

stripes ye were healed," 1 Peter 2:24.

The promise of healing of the body is sure. God made your body, and He alone understands the human body. Doctors and surgeons may do their best. Sometimes, God uses them to restore health and completeness to you. However, you must always look to God for healing. He is not limited in power as doctors are. He can heal known and unknown sicknesses. He doesn't need to examine the cause of a sickness in a lab to create an antidote. God knows the names of past, existing and future sicknesses. Nothing happens without His consent (Acts 15:18; Isaiah 46:10).

He has promised to heal you of all sicknesses, diseases, aches and pain. He will not disappoint you when you ask Him for healing.

God is ever faithful to His word and you must learn to trust Him for healing. You don't need healing in heaven; there is no sickness in heaven. Sicknesses exist only on this earth. So it is enough reason that God is willing to heal you right here and now (Numbers 23:19).

Divine Provisions

"When the poor and needy seek water, and there is none, and their tongue faileth for thirst, I the Lord will hear them, I the God of Israel will not forsake them," Isaiah 41:17.

We have basic needs and God knows we have these needs. He even asked us not to allow worry and anxiety take over our hearts and minds. If He can feed the birds that fly and animals that live on the land and the sea, He can provide for us. Man is the crown of God's creation. God created man in His own image and likeness. He will do anything to make sure man has food, water, shelter and clothing (Matthew 6:26-30; Luke 12:28).

Man is the only reason God still intervenes in the affairs of this world. Man is a precious being, so God is concerned with the wellbeing of man. Man is the only creature that can carry out God's will perfectly. To help man fulfil this important mission, God makes sure He feeds and clothes him.

You are precious to God, "For thus saith the Lord of hosts; After the glory hath he sent me unto the nations which spoiled you: for he that toucheth you toucheth the apple of his eye, Zechariah 2:8.

He has promised to bless you with all the good things of life (Psalm 104:13-15; Judges 9:13). Don't let your mind or the opinion of others make you doubt God's promise of provisions. If God said it, then it is true. If it is true, then He will do it (Psalm 89:35; Isaiah 46:10; Isaiah 55:8-13; Jeremiah 11:5; Ezekiel 34:15; John 14:13-14).

Divine Opportunities and Financial Breakthrough

"Behold, I will do a new thing; now it shall spring forth; shall ye not know it? I will even make a way in the wilderness, and rivers in the desert," Isaiah 43:19.

When God promises you a bright future, no one can stop Him. God knows the way through the maze of difficulties, hardship and unpleasant situations. He created the things we see and the things we do not see (Isaiah 40:26; Colossians 1:16). When He gives a command, situations obey without question. God knows the best things for you. He has the best things for you, and He has promised to do the best things for you (Deuteronomy 26:15; Isaiah 7:22).

When you are looking for something important in a large area, you stand on a high place and look down. Advanced countries used that method to find the people, places and things they need. They use satellites and drones to search for people and things they want. God lives in heaven and is above every living thing. From His abode, He sees everything that happens in the world. He sees the way that leads to juicy opportunities and amazing destinations in life. His promises can guide you to the things you need in this life (Jeremiah 29:11; Proverbs 8:21; Colossians 2:3).

Genesis 26:3
"Sojourn in this land, and I will be with thee, and will bless thee; for unto thee, and unto thy seed, I will give all these countries, and I will perform the oath which I sware unto Abraham thy father."

Divine Protection and Guidance

"When thou passest through the waters, I will be with thee; and through the rivers, they shall not overflow thee: when thou walkest through the fire, thou shalt not be burned; neither shall the flame kindle upon thee," Isaiah 43:2.

God is everywhere and that is big reason you should depend on His protection and guidance. He promised to be with us everywhere we go, in good and bad times. With God by our side, problems fade away and difficult situations lose their seriousness. God makes the path we follow smooth and easy. He teaches us how to be safe from harm and dangers. The protection of God is stronger and difficult to break through. When God is your Protector, nothing can harm you. When God is your Guide, no one can mislead you (Psalm 32:8; Isaiah 58:11; 2 Samuel 22:35; Psalm 18:34; Jeremiah 15:12).

The stories of Abraham, Isaac and Jacob are examples of divine guidance. God promised to go with them in their journey of life. Abraham left his country to a place God promised to give him. As he relied on God's guidance, he became strong, healthy, wealthy and fertile. God led him to a life of plentifulness and fulfilment. Isaac, the direct son of Abraham took after his father. God made him very successful too (Genesis 26:2-5, 13-14), because he relied on God's guidance. Jacob, Isaac's son, prayed for God's guidance and protection (Genesis 28:20-22). God protected him from dangers and prospered him in a land far from home (Genesis 30:43).

God's promise of protection is still in the Bible and available for you. You can pray for His protection or ask Him to guide you as He has promised. God listens to the prayers of His people. He loves to help them reach their goals and life's destinations. If you trust Him, He will guide you through the complex maze of life. God is the owner of all life on earth and

He can handle matters of life and destiny.

Genesis 28:15
"And, behold, I am with thee, and will keep thee in all places whither thou goest, and will bring thee again into this land; for I will not leave thee, until I have done that which I have spoken to thee of."

Matthew 28:20B
"...lo, I am with you alway, even unto the end of the world. Amen.

Summary

God's promises for our physical and material needs are important. They help us to see God as a true Father. A good father would meet the physical needs of the family. If God is our Heavenly Father, He would provide food, water, clothing, shelter, and everything we need. The Bible is filled with so many promises of God concerning our basic needs. God is good and merciful, and wants you to know that He wants to meet your needs every day.

CHAPTER THREE

The Promises We Don't See

2 Corinthians 9:8
"And God is able to make all grace abound toward you; that ye, always having all sufficiency in all things, may abound to every good work."

Ephesians 1:3-4
"Blessed be the God and Father of our Lord Jesus Christ, who hath blessed us with all spiritual blessings in heavenly places in Christ: According as he hath chosen us in him before the foundation of the world, that we should be holy and without blame before him in love."

God wants His work and blessings to first begin from the inside of us.

His spiritual promises are more important for our lives than the physical ones. God wants us to enjoy His spiritual promises as much as we enjoy His physical promises. Our relationship with God begins with the acceptance of a promise we don't yet see.

When God called Abraham, He told him of an unknown land. Abraham had never seen the land of promise. He could only imagine it but could not picture exactly how it looked. He could only depend on God's word and promise. Abraham believed that God was saying the truth, and the joy of it helped him to trust in God's promises (Genesis 12:1; Hebrews 11:8-10).

When Jesus walked on earth, He pointed men and women to the spiritual promises and blessings God had for them. Jesus encouraged His disciples to make sure they were filled with spiritual blessings all the time (John 6:27; 3 John 2). The spiritual blessings in your life make it easy to inherit physical and financial blessings. God's spiritual blessings are so rich and full that they contain all the other blessings you may be looking for.

Ephesians 1:3-4
"Blessed be the God and Father of our Lord Jesus Christ, who hath blessed us with all spiritual blessings in heavenly places in Christ: According as he hath chosen us in him before the foundation of the world, that we should be holy and without blame before him in love."

Satan tempted Jesus and tried to turn His attention to acquiring material things before starting His ministry of soul winning. Jesus knew God's promises. He knew that God has promised His people both physical and spiritual wealth. But Jesus also knew that the spiritual realm rules the physical. Jesus showed us our lives with spiritual blessings first and other blessings will follow (Matthew 4:4; 6:33; Luke 4:4).

God's Spiritual Promises

God's spiritual promises are as numerous and numberless as His physical promises. God is unlimited, so what He can do for us is uncountable (Job 5:9; 9:10). The Bible recorded that what Jesus did were so many that no book could contain them (John 21:25). Think about that: what you get from God are both numberless and limitless. What you can do and achieve through God's grace are uncountable (1 Corinthians 15:10; 2 Corinthians

8:7; 2 Corinthians 9:8; Ephesians 3:8).

You receive all of God's spiritual promises by faith: *"Therefore it is of faith, that it might be by grace; to the end the promise might be sure to all the seed; not to that only which is of the law, but to that also which is of the faith of Abraham; who is the father of us all,"* Romans 4:16.

The Promise of Salvation
"My people, go ye out of the midst of her, and deliver ye every man his soul from the fierce anger of the Lord," Jeremiah 51:45.

"He will turn again, he will have compassion upon us; he will subdue our iniquities; and thou wilt cast all their sins into the depths of the sea," Micah 7:19.

"And she shall bring forth a son, and thou shalt call his name JESUS: for he shall save his people from their sins," Matthew 1:21.

"For by grace are ye saved through faith; and that not of yourselves: it is the gift of God," Ephesians 2:8.

"But God commendeth his love toward us, in that, while we were yet sinners, Christ died for us," Romans 5:8.

"For God hath not appointed us to wrath, but to obtain salvation by our Lord Jesus Christ, [10] Who died for us, that, whether we wake or sleep, we should live together with him," 1 Thessalonians 5:9-10.

These are the promises God made concerning our salvation and redemption. The first man Adam sold us all to Satan through the sin of disobedience (Genesis 3:6-16; Romans 5:14; 1 Corinthians 15:22). Since then, sin became the nature of everyone born into the world. In His love, God did not give up on us. He made a promise to save us from sin and deliver us from the power and prison of the devil (Jeremiah 31:31-34; Hebrews 8:12.

Jesus became the sacrificial Lamb through whom we received our redemption. So always holds on to this promise. God has delivered you from all sin. Your past has been forgiven, and you have grace to enjoy the full benefits of redemption and salvation through Jesus Christ, the Son of God (Psalm 40:6-8; Matthew 1:21; John 19:30; 1 Peter 2:24).

The Promise of Adoption
The nature of man is sin and it is impossible to live for God with the sin nature in us. God is holy and only people of holiness dare come near Him. The angels in heaven are holy beings, which is why they can stand in God's presence. The sinful nature is always against God (Roman's 8:7; James 4:4). We cannot become good by our own strength or efforts. Only God Himself can make us holy enough to come to Him. To make it possible, God made a promise to adopt us as His children. He knew that we had no power to change.

Ephesians 1:5
"Having predestinated us unto the adoption of children by Jesus Christ to himself, according to the good pleasure of his will..."

Romans 8:23

"And not only they, but ourselves also, which have the firstfruits of the Spirit, even we ourselves groan within ourselves, waiting for the adoption, to wit, the redemption of our body."

Galatians 4:5
"To redeem them that were under the law, that we might receive the adoption of sons."

Romans 8:15
"For ye have not received the spirit of bondage again to fear; but ye have received the Spirit of adoption, whereby we cry, Abba, Father."

Praise God! Even before God made us, He knew that a day like this would come. So He devised a way to make us part of His glorious family. He so much loved us that He couldn't allow the devil make us children of darkness.

You are an adopted child of God through Jesus Christ. God is now your Father both on earth and in heaven. You have access to Him just as Jesus Christ and the angel have. You can pray to God and receive answers to your prayers in the name of Jesus Christ (Romans 8:32; John 16:26-27).

The Promise of Peace
Genesis 43:23
Psalm 29:11
"The Lord will give strength unto his people; the Lord will bless his people with peace."

Psalm 37:11
"But the meek shall inherit the earth; and shall delight themselves in the abundance of peace."

Proverbs 16:7
"When a man's ways please the Lord, he maketh even his enemies to be at peace with him."

Isaiah 26:3

"Thou wilt keep him in perfect peace, whose mind is stayed on thee: because he trusteth in thee."

Isaiah 53:5
"But he was wounded for our transgressions, he was bruised for our iniquities: the chastisement of our peace was upon him; and with his stripes we are healed."

John 14:27
"Peace I leave with you, my peace I give unto you: not as the world giveth, give I unto you. Let not your heart be troubled, neither let it be afraid."

God created us to live a peaceful life here on earth. When we lose that peace, life can be so unbearably painful. God foresaw this and promised to give us peace. The peace of God in our hearts helps us live in peace with

God and with other people. When peace is in our hearts, it makes our prayers effective and our words powerful.

Receive the peace God promised you. A world without peace is filled with confusion and chaos. A life without peace will lack joy, love and patience. We need peace to fulfil our earthly and heavenly missions. Peace is one of the foundations of our relationship with God. On it hinges our courage, faith and power to do and receive the will of God (Romans 5:1; Philippians 4:7; Hebrews 12:14).

The Promise of Forgiveness
God has forgotten and forgiven your sins through His Son, Jesus Christ. After the fall of Adam and Eve, no man on earth was qualified to bring humankind

back to God. Only a spotless and sinless person could do it. Unfortunately, there was none who could do that. God decided to save us through His Son Jesus Christ. Jesus, the second person in the Trinity, took on a human form and was born of the virgin Mary. He grew up, spread the message of God's love, and did a lot of healings, miracles and signs and wonders (Matthew 4:23-25; Acts 10:38).

When the time came, Jesus Christ went to the cross to die in our place (Galatians 4:4-5). Everything He did was fully connected with our salvation, redemption, reconciliation and forgiveness (Romans 8:31-34). Today, the promise of forgiveness is yours. You claim it by confessing your sins and accepting everything Jesus did on the cross for you.

Romans 10:9-11

"That if thou shalt confess with thy mouth the Lord Jesus, and shalt believe in thine heart that God hath raised him from the dead, thou shalt be saved. For with the heart man believeth unto righteousness; and with the mouth confession is made unto salvation. For the scripture saith, Whosoever believeth on him shall not be ashamed."

When you confess the Lordship of Christ over your life and surrender your entire life to Him, you receive the promised gift of forgiveness. Forgiveness comes from Jesus Christ. When you make mistakes, don't beat yourself. Tell Jesus what you did and receive His forgiveness immediately.

Daniel 9:9

"To the Lord our God belong mercies and forgivenesses, though we have rebelled against him."

Acts 5:31
"Him hath God exalted with his right hand to be a Prince and a Saviour, for to give repentance to Israel, and forgiveness of sins."

Acts 13:38
"Be it known unto you therefore, men and brethren, that through this man is preached unto you the forgiveness of sins."

Acts 26:18
"To open their eyes, and to turn them from darkness to light, and from the power of Satan unto God, that they may receive forgiveness of sins, and inheritance among them which are sanctified by faith that is in me."

Ephesians 1:7
"In whom we have redemption through his blood, the forgiveness of sins, according to the riches of his grace."

Colossians 1:14
"In whom we have redemption through his blood, even the forgiveness of sins."

God no longer holds your sins against you because of the sacrifice of Jesus Christ. Get rid of the guilt and regrets and receive God's gift of forgiveness. Don't worry too much; God chose to forgive you. It has nothing to do with you; it's God's nature to show mercy and grace to His creatures. Accept His promise of forgiveness by faith and enjoy lifetime benefits of His grace.

Romans 4:16

"Therefore it is of faith, that it might be by grace; to the end the promise might be sure to all the seed; not to that only which is of the law, but to that also which is of the faith of Abraham; who is the father of us all..."

The Promise of Righteousness

Psalm 24:5

"He shall receive the blessing from the Lord, and righteousness from the God of his salvation."

Righteousness is a gift from God. He promised to give righteousness to those who trust and obey Him. God is righteous and only righteous people can come close to Him. Our good behaviors and right conduct cannot qualify us. Man's righteousness is unacceptable to God. We need a higher form of righteousness to be in fellowship with God. This righteousness comes to us as a gift. Through Jesus Christ, shows us mercy and freely made us righteous (Job 15:16; Psalm 53:3; Zechariah 3:1-3; Colossians 3:8).

Only God's kind of righteousness is acceptable. He will never accept anyone who does not have the righteousness of Christ. Knowing that we cannot meet that requirement, God transferred the righteousness of Jesus Christ to us. Believing and accepting Jesus Christ clothe you with God's kind of righteousness.

Isaiah 32:1
"Behold, a king shall reign in righteousness, and princes shall rule in judgment."

Isaiah 42:6
"I the Lord have called thee in righteousness, and will hold thine hand, and will keep thee, and give thee for a covenant of the people, for a light of the Gentiles."

Romans 3:22
"Even the righteousness of God which is by faith of Jesus Christ unto all and upon all them that

believe: for there is no difference."

Romans 5:17
"For if by one man's offence death reigned by one; much more they which receive abundance of grace and of the gift of righteousness shall reign in life by one, Jesus Christ."

Philippians 3:9
"And be found in him, not having mine own righteousness, which is of the law, but that which is through the faith of Christ, the righteousness which is of God by faith."

Philippians 1:11
"Being filled with the fruits of righteousness, which are by Jesus Christ, unto the glory and praise of God."

Romans 4:21-25

"And being fully persuaded that, what he had promised, he was able also to perform. And therefore it was imputed to him for righteousness. Now it was not written for his sake alone, that it was imputed to him; But for us also, to whom it shall be imputed, if we believe on him that raised up Jesus our Lord from the dead; Who was delivered for our offences, and was raised again for our justification."

You have God's righteousness if already you believe in Jesus Christ. You don't need to do anything to get it. It is a gift: God gave it to you without asking for money. It's a promise He made and fulfilled in Jesus Christ

Luke 1:73-75
"The oath which he sware to our father Abraham, That he would grant unto us, that we being

delivered out of the hand of our enemies might serve him without fear, In holiness and righteousness before him, all the days of our life."

The Promise of a New Heart
Ezekiel 36:26
"A new heart also will I give you, and a new spirit will I put within you: and I will take away the stony heart out of your flesh, and I will give you an heart of flesh."

Jeremiah 32:39-40
"And I will give them one heart, and one way, that they may fear me for ever, for the good of them, and of their children after them: And I will make an everlasting covenant with them, that I will not turn away from them, to do them good; but I will put my fear in their hearts, that they shall not depart from me."

A new heart makes you a different person. It helps you to understand God and love Him more. The Lord knows that the heart is the center of life. Once the heart is right, every other thing falls in place. God doesn't want to repair our hearts. Fixing it that way doesn't guarantee a better and stable future. So the best thing was to give us a brand new heart. This new heart is filled with love, peace and joy. It is a heart that comes directly from God through the sacrifice of Christ.

Hebrews 8:10
"For this is the covenant that I will make with the house of Israel after those days, saith the Lord; I will put my laws into their mind, and write them in their hearts: and I will be to them a God, and they shall be to me a people."

Hebrews 10:16
"This is the covenant that I will make with them after those days, saith the Lord, I will put my laws into their hearts, and in their minds will I write them."

Ephesians 3:17
"That Christ may dwell in your hearts by faith; that ye, being rooted and grounded in love."

Galatians 4:6
"And because ye are sons, God hath sent forth the Spirit of his Son into your hearts, crying, Abba, Father."

2 Corinthians 4:6
"For God, who commanded the light to shine out of darkness, hath shined in our hearts, to give the light of the knowledge of the glory of God in the face of Jesus Christ."

The Promise of Eternal Life

Titus 1:2

"In hope of eternal life, which God, that cannot lie, promised before the world began."

1 John 2:25

"And this is the promise that he hath promised us, even eternal life."

God's love for us is so deep and broad that He is willing to give us His own kind of life. Eternal life is the life of God. It is the very life that keeps God forever alive. God cannot die because His life is everlasting. God chose to give us this long lasting life so we can become like Him in nature and character. This eternal life makes us live for the glory of God. Also, we will live forever with God because of this unending life. Jesus Christ paid the price for the promise of eternal life.

John 3:15
"That whosoever believeth in him should not perish, but have eternal life."

Romans 6:23

"For the wages of sin is death; but the gift of God is eternal life through Jesus Christ our Lord."

1 John 1:2

(For the life was manifested, and we have seen it, and bear witness, and shew unto you that eternal life, which was with the Father, and was manifested unto us;)

1 John 5:11

"And this is the record, that God hath given to us eternal life, and this life is in his Son."

1 John 5:20

"And we know that the Son of God is come, and hath given us an understanding, that we may know him that is true, and we are in him that is true, even in his Son Jesus Christ. This is the true God, and eternal life."

The Promise of the Spirit

God promised to give the Holy Spirit to those who believe in Jesus Christ. It is an experience that is supposed to surpass that of Old Testament saints. King David, Hezekiah, Prophets Isaiah, Jeremiah, Daniel, Elijah and Elisha all had the Spirit of God working through them. But the New Testament promise of the Spirit was to fill the heart of believers and help them always. They don't need to sing songs or play musical instruments to connect with the Holy Spirit. Jesus said the Holy Spirit will be in us all the time.

John 14:16-17

"And I will pray the Father, and he shall give you another Comforter, that he may abide with you for ever; [17] Even the Spirit of truth; whom the world

cannot receive, because it seeth him not, neither knoweth him: but ye know him; for he dwelleth with you, and shall be in you."

If you're yet to receive the Holy Spirit, open your heart to God and ask Him to fill your heart with the Holy Spirit. The promise of the Father is for everyone who believes (Acts 2:38-39).

Summary

The spiritual promises and blessings of God are as real as His physical and material ones. God wants you to have both His spiritual and physical blessings. He made these promises to you long before you were born. Jesus died so He could make these spiritual promises real to you (2 Corinthians 1:20; Ephesians 3:6; Hebrews 10:38). Claim them and walk in them by the faith of Jesus

Christ (Romans 4:16; Galatians 2:20).

CHAPTER FOUR

Why God Made Promises

All the riches of the world cannot buy even one promise of God. The promises of God are so precious that money cannot buy them. No human can purchase them, and God knows that. It is impossible to even try to pay for them. Just as man has no power to save himself, so man cannot buy the promises of God. The Lord decided to help His creatures by freely giving us these promises and blessings.

Psalm 105:20
"The king sent and loosed him; even the ruler of the people, and let him go free."

Hosea 14:4

"I will heal their backsliding, I will love them freely: for mine anger is turned away from him."

Romans 3:24

"Being justified freely by his grace through the redemption that is in Christ Jesus:"

Romans 8:32

"He that spared not his own Son, but delivered him up for us all, how shall he not with him also freely give us all things?"

God's love drives Him to do anything for us. His physical and spiritual promises are so numerous that no one can count them. But why did God give us all these precious promises without demanding anything?

Here are the reasons:

God is our Creator

Genesis 1:27

"So God created man in his own image, in the image of God created he him; male and female created he them."

Psalm 148:5

"Let them praise the name of the Lord: for he commanded, and they were created."

Colossians 1:16

"For by him were all things created, that are in heaven, and that are in earth, visible and invisible, whether they be thrones, or dominions, or principalities, or powers: all things were created by him, and for him:"

God created us to think, act and live like Him. He is our able Provider, Comforter and Healer. He wants to take care of all our needs just as parents look after their children. It is a duty He chooses to do despite our human weaknesses.

God is our Father

Psalm 89:26
"He shall cry unto me, Thou art my father, my God, and the rock of my salvation."

Psalm 27:10
"When my father and my mother forsake me, then the Lord will take me up."

God becomes your Father when you accept Jesus as your older brother. God is the spiritual Father of all believers in Christ. If you have no one to call your father, God promised to be your Father. He wants you to tell Him your needs and enjoy His promised blessings. Only God can do what other fathers cannot do.

His promises are yours because He is your Father and you are His child.

God is Good
Luke 18:19
"And Jesus said unto him, Why callest thou me good? none is good, save one, that is, God."

God is the source of all goodness. It is His nature to think and do well to everyone. God sees the evil in the world, yet He sends rain and sunlight on earth. He hears the wrong thoughts in our hearts but chooses to show us mercy instead. God's goodness prevents Him from punishing us for all the bad things we do almost all the time. God's goodness remains an inseparable part of His nature (1 Chronicles 16:34; Psalm 27:13; Matthew 5:44-48).

God is Love

When you love someone, you help them and comfort them when they need it. God loves us, so He gave us all these promises and blessings. He cannot stand to watch us suffer from sickness, poverty and darkness. His heart of love wants the best for us in all things.

1 John 4:8
"He that loveth not knoweth not God; for God is love."

1 John 4:11-12
"Beloved, if God so loved us, we ought also to love one another. No man hath seen God at any time. If we love one another, God dwelleth in us, and his love is perfected in us."

1 John 4:19
"We love him, because he first loved us."

God is Merciful

Exodus 15:13

"Thou in thy mercy hast led forth the people which thou hast redeemed: thou hast guided them in thy strength unto thy holy habitation."

Exodus 34:6-7

"And the Lord passed by before him, and proclaimed, The Lord, The Lord God, merciful and gracious, longsuffering, and abundant in goodness and truth, Keeping mercy for thousands, forgiving iniquity and transgression and sin, and that will by no means clear the guilty; visiting the iniquity of the fathers upon the children, and upon the children's children, unto the third and to the fourth generation."

God's mercy saves and emancipates us. God's mercy protects us from the power of

Satan and his evil powers. Every day, we live by God's mercy (Lamentation 3:23; Romans 9:15; 2 Corinthians 4:1; 1 Timothy 1:16; 1 Peter 1:3). When we learn to hold on to God by His nature of mercy, we will easily come out of many problems we encounter in life.

God is God
Leviticus 25:38
"I am the Lord your God, which brought you forth out of the land of Egypt, to give you the land of Canaan, and to be your God."

Isaiah 45:22
"Look unto me, and be ye saved, all the ends of the earth: for I am God, and there is none else."

One big reason God gave us precious promises is because He is God. He is the Supreme Being who existed before the world came to be. God is everywhere because He is God and that's what God does. God can do anything and everything. He can change lives in the split of a second. God can save, heal and restore lost blessings. Since He can do all things, He decided to promise us the good things of life.

Malachi 3:6
"For I am the Lord, I change not; therefore ye sons of Jacob are not consumed."

God is Powerful

Jeremiah 32:27
"Behold, I am the Lord, the God of all flesh: is there any thing too hard for me?"

Matthew 19:26
"But Jesus beheld them, and said unto them, With men this is impossible; but with God all things are possible."

Mark 10:27

"And Jesus looking upon them saith, With men it is impossible, but not with God: for with God all things are possible."

God has power over all visible and invisible things. No one can challenge God in a battle and win. No demon or sickness can stand before Him. God's power is limitless and comprehensive. There's no life it cannot reach, and there's no problem it cannot solve. He wants to use that power to work wonders in our lives. Therefore, He made promises to us; promises that demonstrate His power over all things.

Summary

In your relationship and journey with God, you will hit a rough spot. Sometimes, it comes in the form of doubt, sickness or sadness. Remember that God is not far away. He is ever ready to fulfil His promises. Look at all the reasons why God is willing to help you: He is your Creator, Father, and God. He is a God of love, mercy and goodness. Let these qualities and duties of God cheer you up every day.

CHAPTER FIVE

The Enemies of God's Promises

Luke 1:74-75
"That he would grant unto us, that we being delivered out of the hand of our enemies might serve him without fear, In holiness and righteousness before him, all the days of our life."

We have God's promises on one hand, and we have enemies of these promises on the other. These enemies want to take from us the things we receive from God. The Bible tells us that deliverance from these enemies will ensure our victory.

You must identity these enemies and stop them before they stop or limit your blessings. God's blessings cover every area of our lives. We need them all to enjoy a perfectly fulfilled life in Christ. Jesus paid the price for the inheritance to be ours. His death signed and sealed the covenant promises.

Hebrews 7:22
"By so much was Jesus made a surety of a better testament."

Hebrews 9:15
"And for this cause he is the mediator of the new testament, that by means of death, for the redemption of the transgressions that were under the first testament, they which are called might receive the promise of eternal inheritance."

Hebrews 10:13-14

"From henceforth expecting till his enemies be made his footstool. For by one offering he hath perfected for ever them that are sanctified."

The Five Enemies of God's Promises

1. Sin and Disobedience

The problem between God and man are sin and disobedience. Sin disqualifies us from the promises of God. When we identify the sin we are struggling with and repent of it, God's promises come alive to us. We must get rid of the real problem between us and God or we may never enjoy much of God's goodness.

Proverbs 14:34
"Righteousness exalteth a nation: but sin is a reproach to any people."

Isaiah 59:1-2

"Behold, the Lord's hand is not shortened, that it cannot save; neither his ear heavy, that it cannot hear: But your iniquities have separated between you and your God, and your sins have hid his face from you, that he will not hear."

Jeremiah 5:25
"Your iniquities have turned away these things, and your sins have withholden good things from you."

Deuteronomy 28:2
"And all these blessings shall come on thee, and overtake thee, if thou shalt hearken unto the voice of the Lord thy God."

2. Lack of Faith

Faith is the key to God's storehouses of blessings. God's promises are unlimited and He can fulfill all of them in your lifetime. Knowing these promises is the beginning, but having the faith to make them yours is important. A lack of faith in God robs you of the blessings of these promises.

Isaiah 53:1
"Who hath believed our report? and to whom is the arm of the Lord revealed?"

Matthew 8:13
And Jesus said unto the centurion, Go thy way; and as thou hast believed, so be it done unto thee. And his servant was healed in the selfsame hour.

2 Corinthians 4:13
We having the same spirit of faith, according as it is written, I believed, and therefore have I spoken; we also believe, and therefore speak;

Matthew 21:21-22

"Jesus answered and said unto them, Verily I say unto you, If ye have faith, and doubt not, ye shall not only do this which is done to the fig tree, but also if ye shall say unto this mountain, Be thou removed, and be thou cast into the sea; it shall be done. And all things, whatsoever ye shall ask in prayer, believing, ye shall receive."

3. Absence of Prayer

Prayer is an important part of the Christian life. We talk to God through prayer. We tell God our needs and desires through prayer. Prayer helps us to stay alive spiritually. A lack of prayer will find us walking in darkness. We mention God's promises to Him when we pray. If we don't pray, we have no other way to claim the promises of God.

Deuteronomy 32:1
"Give ear, O ye heavens, and I will speak; and hear, O earth, the words of my mouth."

Zechariah 10:1
"Ask ye of the Lord rain in the time of the latter rain; so the Lord shall make bright clouds, and give them showers of rain, to every one grass in the field."

Matthew 7:7-8
"Ask, and it shall be given you; seek, and ye shall find; knock, and it shall be opened unto you: [8] For every one that asketh receiveth; and he that seeketh findeth; and to him that knocketh it shall be opened."

4. Ignorance of God's Promises

The more of God's promises you know, the richer your prayer life. God's word in your mouth makes your life powerful and full of God's blessings. If you don't read or study the Bible, you will have no promise to claim. The Bible contains all the promises you will ever need.

Joshua 1:8
"This book of the law shall not depart out of thy mouth; but thou shalt meditate therein day and night, that thou mayest observe to do according to all that is written therein: for then thou shalt make thy way prosperous, and then thou shalt have good success."

John 5:39-40
"Search the scriptures; for in them ye think ye have eternal life: and they are they which testify of me. And ye will not come to me, that ye might have life."

2 Timothy 2:15
"Study to shew thyself approved unto God, a workman that needeth not to be ashamed, rightly dividing the word of truth."

5. Impatience

Although God is powerful and His promises are true, you still need a good deal of patience. Some prayers work the moment you say them. Sometimes, a promise takes a while to fulfil. When God promised a son to Abraham, he waited 25 years to see it. The nature of the promise you are waiting for determines how long you wait. So don't lose faith, but be patient and keep waiting for the promise to manifest.

Psalm 27:13-14
"I had fainted, unless I had believed to see the goodness of the Lord in the land of the living. [14] Wait on the Lord: be of good courage, and he shall strengthen thine heart: wait, I say, on the Lord."

Romans 4:18

"Who against hope believed in hope, that he might become the father of many nations; according to that which was spoken, So shall thy seed be."

Hebrews 6:12
"That ye be not slothful, but followers of them who through faith and patience inherit the promises."

Summary

The promises of God are as reliable as God Himself. You can trust them to work for you and transform your life in line with God's intentions. God cannot lie and His word are reliable. When God makes promises, He will fulfil them. When He fulfills them, your faith increases and you trust Him more.

You should look out for the five enemies of faith. Sin comes first and can neutralize and delay God's promises. If you know what God promised, you can claim them in prayer and patiently wait for the fulfilment of His word in your life and family.

Thank God for His love, grace and mercy. He has given us precious promises to go through life victoriously and prosperously through Jesus Christ. Believe, claim and you will receive the manifestations of these promises from Him.